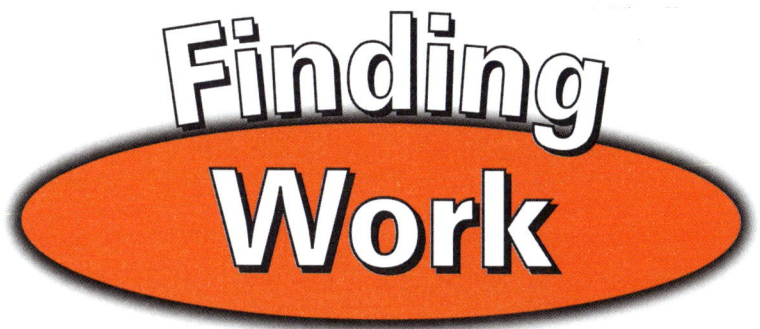

by Stuart Schwartz and Craig Conley

Content Consultant:
Robert J. Miller, Ph.D.
Associate Professor
Mankato State University

CAPSTONE
HIGH/LOW BOOKS
an imprint of Capstone Press

C A P S T O N E   P R E S S
818 North Willow Street • Mankato, MN 56001
http://www.capstone-press.com

Copyright © 1998 Capstone Press. All rights reserved.
No part of this book may be reproduced without written permission from the publisher.
The publisher takes no responsibility for the use of any of the materials
or methods described in this book, nor for the products thereof.
Printed in the United States of America.

Library of Congress Cataloging-in-Publication Data
Schwartz, Stuart, 1945-
    Finding work/by Stuart Schwartz and Craig Conley.
    p. cm. -- (Looking at work)
    Includes bibliographical references and index.
    Summary: Examines different kinds of jobs and explores ways of finding appropriate employment.
    ISBN 1-56065-713-8
    1. Job hunting--Juvenile literature.
[1. Job hunting. 2. Vocational guidance.] I. Conley, Craig, 1965-   . II. Title.
III. Series: Schwartz, Stuart, 1945-   Looking at work.
HF5382.7.S39 1998
650.14 21--dc21
                                                       97-52334
                                                          CIP
                                                          AC

Photo credits:
All photos by Dede Smith Photography

Table of Contents

Chapter 1 Finding Work 5
Chapter 2 Skills and Experience 7
Chapter 3 Choosing a Job 9
Chapter 4 Help-Wanted Ads 11
Chapter 5 Placing Ads 13
Chapter 6 Personal Contacts 15
Chapter 7 Job Counselors 17
Chapter 8 Employment Agencies 19
Chapter 9 Temporary Agencies 21
Chapter 10 Programs for Students 23
Chapter 11 Issues to Think About 25
Chapter 12 You Can Find Work 27

Words to Know 28
To Learn More 29
Useful Addresses 30
Internet Sites 31
Index 32

Chapter 1

Finding Work

Many people think finding work is hard. Looking for work can be hard. But there are many ways to make a job search easier.

A person who is looking for work can find help in many places. Most communities have programs and services that help people find work. Newspapers list jobs that are available. Companies often list job openings on the Internet. Friends and family members can help.

Creating a plan can make finding work easier. People should think about the skills and experience they have. They should also think about the kinds of jobs they would like. People should then gather information about the kinds of jobs that interest them. Information is facts and ideas.

Job seekers can gather information by visiting state employment offices. They can look up information at libraries. They can also contact employers directly. People can begin searching for jobs after they have gathered all the information they need.

People looking for work can find help in many places.

Chapter 2

Skills and Experience

Job seekers should look for work that is right for them. Job seekers should think about their skills and experience.

People learn skills in many ways. For example, people who build model airplanes must fit together small parts. Building model airplanes teaches people how to work with their hands. That skill might help model airplane builders get jobs manufacturing computers. Other people might enjoy cooking at home. They like to learn new ways to prepare food. People who enjoy cooking may have the skills necessary to work as cooks.

People can gain experience in many ways, too. For example, people who baby-sit learn how to care for children. They learn to be patient when children are difficult. Baby-sitters also learn to be responsible. Responsible means being trustworthy and dependable. Baby-sitting helps people gain the experience needed to work in child care centers.

People learn skills and gain experience in many ways.

Chapter 3

Choosing a Job

People must think about their career goals when choosing job fields. Career goals are plans for future work. People also need to gather information about the kinds of jobs that interest them. For example, they need to learn how much experience and training jobs require. They also need to know how much jobs pay.

People can gather information about jobs in many places. Public libraries have job information. Community job services also offer information about jobs. Job services are listed in the Yellow Pages under Employment or Jobs. The Yellow Pages is a section in a phone book that lists businesses by subject. People can contact employers for job information, too.

Other people in communities can be sources of information. For example, someone interested in being a police officer could talk to a police officer. Students can visit guidance counselors. Guidance counselors help students learn about jobs and plan careers. Job counselors offer this information to people who are not students.

People can gather information about jobs in many places.

Help-Wanted Ads

Most job seekers look in help-wanted ads. Help-wanted ads appear in the classified sections of newspapers. Many employers place help-wanted ads in newspapers when they want to hire people.

Help-wanted ads often list information about the skills needed for certain jobs. Sometimes ads list jobs' duties and salaries. Ads also tell job seekers how to contact employers. Ads have phone numbers or addresses. Many ads ask applicants to send resumes. A resume is a summary of a person's experience, job skills, and education.

Newspapers list similar kinds of help-wanted ads in groups. They list the groups alphabetically by job title. For example, someone who wants to work at a child care center should look under Child Care. Titles of jobs and job groups may be different in different newspapers. Some newspapers might list child care jobs under Baby-Sitting or Day Care.

Help-wanted ads are in newspapers.

Chapter 5

Placing Ads

Job seekers also can place ads in newspapers. They place their ads in the Work Wanted or Job Wanted section. The ads state what kind of jobs people want. People list their work experience and skills in ads. They also list telephone numbers or addresses so employers can contact them.

People also can advertise their services in newspapers. For example, a person may have experience doing yard work in his neighborhood. He can advertise his services as a yard worker. Another person might have kept business records for a family member. She can advertise bookkeeping services.

Some people advertise their services in newspapers.

Chapter 6

Personal Contacts

Personal contacts can help people look for work. A personal contact is anyone job seekers know who might help them find work.

Friends and family members are good personal contacts. They know job seekers well. Teachers are also good personal contacts.

Other people can be personal contacts, too. Job seekers can meet personal contacts at many organizations.

Personal contacts can help job seekers choose jobs. They can also tell job seekers about jobs that are available. These may be jobs at their own places of work. Personal contacts may also hear of job openings from their friends.

People who are looking for work should tell their friends, family and acquaintances. Personal contacts can give job seekers useful information and ideas.

Friends and family members are good personal contacts.

Job Counselors

Choosing a job field and finding work can be hard work. Job counselors help people who are having trouble choosing or finding jobs. Many job counselors work for community job services.

Job counselors help people decide which jobs are right for them. Job counselors ask people questions. They ask people what they like to do. Counselors talk with people about their skills and experience.

Job counselors also use tests to help people find job fields that interest them. The tests are not difficult. They help people learn more about themselves. The tests show people which jobs match their interests, skills, and experience.

Job counselors also help people find work after they have chosen a type of job. Employers often contact job counselors to tell them about job opportunities.

Job counselors help people look for work.

Employment Agencies

Employment agencies are businesses or government groups that help people find jobs. Employment agencies keep lists of jobs. People can look at the lists and apply for jobs that interest them.

Every state has a public employment agency. Its services are free. Some counties and cities also have employment agencies. Private employment agencies offer job seekers help, too. People must pay for services at private employment agencies. Sometimes job seekers pay. Sometimes employers pay.

The Yellow Pages lists employment agencies. Employment agencies usually appear under Employment or Job Service. Many employment agencies also place ads in newspapers. Job seekers can find employment agency ads in help-wanted sections.

The Yellow Pages lists employment agencies.

Chapter 9

Temporary Agencies

Some employment agencies are temporary agencies. Temporary agencies help people find temporary jobs. Temporary jobs last for a set amount of time. Employers decide how long temporary jobs will last before they hire temporary workers. Some temporary jobs last for only one day. Others last for a month or a year.

Temporary jobs have some advantages. People can gain good experience at temporary jobs. Temporary jobs are good for people who want to work only a short time. Sometimes temporary jobs can lead to permanent jobs. A permanent job is a position that does not have a set time to end.

Temporary jobs also have disadvantages. They usually do not pay benefits. A benefit is a payment or service in addition to a salary or wages. Temporary workers must find other jobs when temporary jobs end.

Some agencies help people find temporary jobs.

Chapter 10

Programs for Students

Colleges and some high schools offer work-study programs for their students. Work-study programs offer students jobs. Students often get jobs related to the subjects they are studying. For example, an art student might get a work-study job in an art museum.

Many colleges and universities have internship programs. Internships pair students with skilled workers. The students learn valuable skills and gain experience on the job. For example, a photography student might work with a photographer. Internships last for short periods of time. Internships sometimes lead to permanent jobs.

Vocational schools also have work programs. Vocational schools offer classes in skilled trades such as construction, printing, and carpentry. Vocational schools can help some students become apprentices. An apprentice is someone who learns a trade by working with skilled workers. Apprentices earn wages and work regular hours.

Internships help people learn new job skills.

Chapter 11

Advantages and Disadvantages

People who are looking for work have many things to consider. Every job has advantages and disadvantages. For example, construction jobs pay well. But construction jobs might be hard on workers' bodies. Most teachers do not work during summer. But they may have to work extra hours during the school year.

A job seeker might find a job located far away. The job seeker would need to relocate to take the job. Relocate means moving to another place for a job. Relocating might mean moving a family. It might also mean leaving family and friends.

People also must think about traveling to jobs. Workers must be able to get to their jobs on time. For example, a painter learns about a job at a painting company. But the painting company works on homes far from where the painter lives. The painter might have to look for another job if the painter does not have a way to get there.

A worker might need to move to get a job.

Chapter 12

You Can Find Work

Finding work can be hard. But you can make it easier. The first step is deciding what kind of job suits you. Think about your interests, skills, and experience. Choose a job that you can do. Then gather information about that kind of job. Libraries and guidance counselors can help. Get help from a job counselor if you need it.

The next step is finding jobs and applying for them. Look at the help-wanted ads in your newspaper. Tell personal contacts that you are looking for work. Use the job services in your community. Use employment agencies. They can help you find out about job openings. These steps should help you succeed in your job search.

You can succeed in your job search.

Words to Know

apprentice (uh-PREN-tiss)—a person who learns a trade by working with skilled workers

employment agencies (em-PLOI-ment AY-juhn-seez)—businesses or government groups that help people find jobs

help-wanted ad (HELP-WONT-uhd AD)—an advertisement placed in a newspaper by an employer seeking to hire a worker

internship (IN-turn-ship)—a temporary job in which a person works with and learns from skilled workers

relocate (ree-LOH-kate-ing)—to move to another place for a job

resume (REZ-uh-may)—a summary of a person's experience, job skills, and education.

temporary (TEM-puh-rer-ee)—lasting for a set amount of time

work-study program (WURK-STUH-dee PROH-gram)—a program that offers students jobs with flexible hours

To Learn More

Anema, Durlynn. *Get Hired! Finding Job Opportunities*. Hayward, Calif.: Janus, 1990.

Miller, Maryann. *Your Best Foot Forward: Winning Strategies for the Job Interview*. New York: Rosen Publishing Group, 1994.

Schwartz, Stuart and Craig Conley. *Interviewing for a Job*. Looking at Work. Mankato, Minn.: Capstone High/Low Books, 1998.

Useful Addresses

Canada WorkInfoNet
Room 2161, Asticou Training Centre
241 Boulevard Citè des Jeunes
Hull, Quebec K1A 0M7
Canada

Employment and Training Administration
200 Constitution Avenue, NW
Room N-4700
Washington, DC 20210

Jobs for Youth
312 West 36th Street
Suite 600
New York, NY 10001

U.S. Department of Labor
Office of Public Affairs
200 Constitution Avenue NW
Room S-1032
Washington, DC 20210

Internet Sites

America's Job Bank
http://www.ajb.dni.us/

Career Search
http://learningedge.sympatico.ca/careersearch/

CoolWorks
http://www.coolworks.com

Index

apprentice, 23

benefits, 21

career goal, 9

employment agencies, 19, 21, 27

experience, 5, 7, 9, 11, 13, 17, 21, 23, 27

guidance counselor, 9, 27

help-wanted ad, 11, 27

internship, 23

job counselor, 9, 17, 27

relocate, 25

student, 9, 23

temporary agencies, 21

temporary job, 21

vocational school, 23

work-study job, 23

Yellow Pages, 9, 19